Notebook of Love

10 Lessons on Love

@TheNoteboook

Library of Congress Cataloging-in-Publication Data

Tony A. Gaskins Jr.,
@TheNoteboook Twitter
Notebook of Love: 10 Lessons on Love
Published by: Soul Writers, LLC: PO Box 291835 Tampa, Fl 33687

Library of Congress Control Number: 2011918385

ISBN: 978-0-9844822-2-1
"10 9 8 7 6 5 4 3 2 1,"
Printed in the United States of America

Note: This book is intended only as an informative guide for those wishing to know about love. Readers are advised to consult a professional relationship coach or counselor before making any changes in their love life. The reader assumes all responsibility for the consequences of any actions taken based on the information presented in this book. The information in this book is based on the author's research and experience. Every attempt has been made to ensure that the information is accurate; however, the author cannot accept liability for any errors that may exist. The facts and theories on love and relationships are subject to interpretation, and the conclusions and recommendations presented here may not agree with other interpretations.

This book is dedicated to every last person out
there in search of everlasting love and eternal happiness.

I hope the message in this book touches you and helps guide you
on a more informed journey for this crazy thing we call LOVE.

Lastly, to MY true love, SPP; thank you.
~@TheNoteboook

Table of Contents

Love is a learned behavior.

If you don't know love you can't show love.

~Tony Gaskins Jr.

❧1❧

Understanding love

Many people ask, *what is love?* Love is the most difficult thing in the world to explain. No one can clarify all that love is because it's a concept that will be a little different for each person who experiences it. But one can say what love *isn't*. Love is that feeling you feel after the lust is gone yet you still want to spend your every waking moment with that person. Love is the feeling that will make you put someone else before yourself long after you've already won their heart. Love is the reason you sacrifice your time for someone long after the honeymoon stage has ended. Love is pure. Love is passionate. Love is forgiving. Love is giving. Love understands. Love is consuming. Love is uncontrollable. Love encompasses all of those things and more.

Contrary to popular belief, love isn't pain. To say love is pain is an oxymoron in itself. Love is the opposite of pain. Love is the enemy of pain. Love is what conquers pain. Love doesn't hurt; it heals. Those who say that love is pain were most likely hurt while in a relationship, but it's important for you to understand that just because you were in a relationship does not mean that you were in love. Not all love is in a relationship and not all relationships are comprised of love. Know the difference between love and lust. Love warms while lust burns. Lust can lead to a relationship, but that does not guarantee

3

it will lead to love. There is a difference between the two. When you come to this realization, everything you thought you knew about love will evolve.

Love heals us and helps make us whole. Love is the comfort to the pain that life brings. Love is that thing we run to when we can't bear all the pain in the world. Love doesn't expose us; it is our shelter. Never let someone tell you that love is pain. What they are really saying is that they are getting ready to hurt you and they want you to just deal with it and label it love. I know love sounds like a fairytale, but that's the beauty of it. Love is supposed to be that one true feeling we all can experience in our lives. In a world so cruel and cold, we need something warm and tender and that is love.

There was once a young lady who entered her first serious relationship in college only to realize that in this relationship, "love" would be defined to her. It started out as just a friendship with a really handsome guy. He would visit her dorm everyday and she would order food. Some nights, he spent the night, but he never attempted to be intimate with her. He would simply hold her through the night and make sure she fell asleep first. He visited everyday and they spent hours and hours together. This carried on for about three months, and she began to fall in love. She had never met a guy so sweet, kind and understanding. She doubted that he would ever initiate a real relationship or intimacy, so she decided to make a move. One night while at a party, she walked up to him and kissed him. That night, they made the decision to be a couple. Everything was going great for a few months and then the guy began to change. He started to dictate how she should dress, who she could hang out with, and where she was not allowed to hang out. He began pressuring her to cut off friends and family, convincing her that they did not have her best interest at heart the way he did.

This all seemed strange to her but because he was so nice and kind in the beginning, she believed that he had only good intentions. She obeyed him and started distancing herself from friends and family. She spent all of her time with him. She thought it was cute when he put his foot down to tell her that she couldn't go out and party. She saw nothing wrong with his discontent when he saw her speaking to another guy. She felt protected, appreciated and loved. At least that's what she thought was love. It wasn't long before she started to feel depressed. She had been a very social person, but her social life had been brought to a halt by her boyfriend. She was yearning for some time with the girls but he wouldn't grant it to her. He cut off all of his friends as well, but it did not seem to bother him at all. He wanted to be with her every second of the day. Anytime they could not be together, he would grow very angry. He bought her a cell phone so that he could talk to her at all times and so that she could check in with him whenever she had to go somewhere.

She was being herself the best she could, and it would disturb him. He continued trying to change the way she talked, walked, dressed and everything else about her. In his mind, he wanted a particular type of woman, and instead of going to find her, he wanted to transform this young lady into that woman. She was uncomfortable with this predicament, but she figured this behavior was just part of a typical relationship. She wasn't alone because several of her friends were dealing with the same type of guys so she was beginning to believe that this was normal.

A little more than a year into the relationship, he began exploding when he would get angry. He had become a control freak. One night when she called her sister, he felt like she was on the phone too long. Her conversation wasn't pleasing to him so he took the phone and broke it in half. She was shocked and afraid but she interpreted it as love because she thought his actions meant he really cared for her and wanted her all to himself. From there it went to pushing, pulling, slapping, cursing and so on. She found herself in an abusive relationship. This can't be love!

She found herself very confused because this relationship that started out so beautiful had become so full of pain. She had been lulled into this toxic relationship and tricked to believe that this was what love was supposed to be. In truth, this wasn't love at all. This was the self-hate of one individual being imposed onto another and labeled love. She didn't know love so this was her first impression of what love was and this would lead her to say, "Love is pain."

That story serves as an example of how individuals grow to believe that love is pain. If you don't know love, someone may come along and teach you how to hate yourself and ultimately, you will confuse the two!

The moral is that we should all take the time to learn what love is before we enter relationships. Even after starting a relationship, if it starts to hurt every day, be strong enough to pull away from it. Let go so you both can grow! Don't allow yourself to endure this pain hoping that things will change. Instead, make the changes and then the things will change. If you stay in the relationship, they will forever stay the same. Letting go does not mean you will never reconcile, but it does mean that you are strong and smart enough to let go. By letting go, you end the toxic behavior and send a message that says, "I love myself more than this relationship." You should not reenter the relationship unless that person has changed for the better and proven for at least a month to be a new person who handles situations in a different manner. Oftentimes, a toxic person will beg and plead to have you back and swear that they have changed only for you to find out that they are still the same. If that's the case and you have to leave a second time, make up your mind that you will never make the same mistake again. Everyone deserves a second chance because people do have the ability to grow and change, but that is not an excuse to keep playing the fool. Take a stand for the love of yourself and do not waiver in your stance. If you don't love you, then no one will!

If you can identify with the story above, take some time to think. Be honest with yourself and don't step into a ditch with full knowledge that it's there. Never confuse pain for love. The two are not the same and have nothing in common. Although love is one of the hardest things to explain, I hope this helps you get a better understanding.

∽2∽
Loving yourself

What is "loving yourself?" So many people confuse "loving yourself" with pampering yourself. Going to get a manicure or a back massage does not necessarily mean that you love yourself. It could be an expression of love for yourself but it in itself does not mean you love yourself. Many people with low self-esteem do those very things in an attempt to cover up or mask pain and insecurities, but deep down, they lack true love for themselves. Many people go shopping every day or every week in an effort to buy self-worth or class. They aim to fill this void with shopping. They get a temporary high or feel like all their worries have been washed away as long as they have shopping bags. Then not long after the shopping trip is over, they feel down and depressed once again. Loving you goes much deeper than pampering yourself. Loving yourself is not just an expression. It's a belief system. It's a state of mind.

What does it REALLY mean to love you?

Loving yourself means that you know your worth. Loving yourself means that you know how you want to be treated and how you should be treated. Loving yourself means that you do not compromise your beliefs for anyone. Loving yourself means that you do not lower your standards based on circumstance or situation. Loving yourself means that you do not have to be heard before you are seen. Loving yourself means that you do not have to buy your weight in gold just to feel like somebody. Loving yourself means that you are comfortable in your own company and in your own skin. Loving yourself means that you, and not the world around you, define your own beauty. Loving yourself means that you are confident, not conceited. Loving yourself means that you are humble, not haughty. Loving yourself means that you are humble, not arrogant. Loving yourself means that you can share the spotlight. Loving yourself means that you don't have to put others down to build yourself up. Loving yourself means that you are willing to wait no matter how long it takes to get what you are worth. Loving yourself means that you and only you set the standards for your own life. Loving yourself means that you are not willing to lose yourself trying to help someone else find themselves. Loving yourself means that you are strong, but not overbearing. Loving yourself means that you are a leader, not a follower. Loving yourself means that you know what you want and you are willing to do what it takes to get it. Loving yourself means that you are a true friend. Loving yourself means that you are strong enough to let go of a bad situation in order to grow. Loving yourself means that you don't have to argue to get your point across. Loving yourself means that you understand you are beautiful and wonderfully made and that everyone around you is just as beautiful. You see loving yourself is so much more than just an expression.

You have to love yourself before someone else can love you.

It is impossible to accept true love from someone else if you haven't first given it to yourself. You teach others how to treat you by how you treat yourself. If a man is trying to love a woman but she is insecure, broken-hearted and torn on the inside, she will subconsciously push him away. If that man happens to be a weak man himself, then he will recognize her weakness and then exploit that weakness. Since he is a weak man, he will not want to be weak alone. So he will use his size stature and demeanor to break that woman down and bring her beneath him. That weak man will want a weaker being to make him feel stronger. He will debase in an attempt to exalt himself. He will make her feel like less than a person so that he can at least feel like a person. If that woman has not realized that she is failing to love herself, then she will fall victim to this ploy and may never leave this toxic relationship.

On the other hand, if a woman loves herself, she will recognize this man's weakness and stop him before he even gets started. She will possess the strength to tell him that he is weak and that the relationship cannot and will not work. She will let him go so that he can grow. This woman walking away from this weak man will teach him a priceless lesson that could very much change his life and the way he views himself. This man may never be the same after this type of rejection. Then when this strong self-loving woman leaves this weak man, she will attract a real man who sees her love for herself and appreciates it.

By loving yourself, you show others that you know your worth, you know what you want and that you refuse to settle for less. When a strong woman meets a man, that man immediately knows that if he wants this woman to be his, he has to increase his level of confidence and rise up to her level. He can see that she knows her value so he must be willing to grant her that or keep it moving. He knows that he is unable to yell at her, curse at her, mistreat her, disrespect her or cheat on her. He will see her as a queen and he will have to become a king in order to please her. You teach a person how to treat you by how you treat yourself. You set the standard for others to follow. If they measure below that standard, then find the strength to inform them that it would be best for both parties to let it go.

A business deal can be used as an analogy. Imagine applying at a job where the minimum salary should be $10/hour but they offer you $5/hour. If you don't know your worth or the worth of this position, then you will accept the offer only to realize later that you have been cheated. The same concept applies to relationships. If you don't know your value, then you will never get what you're worth, only to realize one day that you've been drained for all you had.

In one instance, there was once a lady who had no idea what a relationship really was all about and she had to learn by trial and error. She met a man and let him lead the way. He aimed to give her everything. He wanted to respect her, but he didn't know all too well himself how to do so. So he tried his luck. He began by picking her up and not opening her door. She ran to get her own door and got in the car. He felt like he was supposed to do it for her but she insisted that she could do it herself, considering how she jumped a step ahead of him to grab her own door. Then when they approached the entrance of the restaurant, she pranced forward and grabbed the door again. He was caught off guard but didn't comment on her actions. In her mind, she wanted to open her own doors to show him she wasn't weak. Although she wanted him to perceive her this way, he interpreted it differently. He saw her as insecure and so desperate for love that she was willing to compromise her self-worth to get a man. He was taken aback, but decided that since she didn't know her worth, then he wouldn't tell her.

After they finished the meal, he asked for the check. He wanted to pay for the check but at the same time, he knew she may have a trick up her sleeve and let her insecurities speak. Sure enough, when the check hit the table, she grabbed it and said, *"I got it."* He tried to stop her and assure her that he would take care of the bill, but she insisted that she could pay it. She told him that she was not like other women and that she could do for a man and also takes care of herself. She thought that she was sending a good message, but to a real man, she was showing her insecurities. He allowed her to pay. After the meal, he was expecting to simply drop her off, give her a hug and a kiss on the cheek and head home. Instead, when they returned to her place, she took the initiative and invited him in. She thought she was being nice and would invite him in to show that she was comfortable with him and was not an uptight female. He perceived her as being frisky and desiring to have sex with him. After they got inside and conversed for about thirty minutes he leaned in to steal a kiss. He felt like it may have been inappropriate, but he did it anyway to test her will. She hadn't really planned on kissing him, but to back up the perception that she wasn't uptight, she allowed him to go for it. Naturally, he went to the next level by trying to undress her. She was uncomfortable but she felt guilty because she did invite him in and now realized that she sent the wrong message. She didn't want to push him away or to make him feel that she was a tease. She was worried about sending mixed messages, so she allowed him to undress her and then they went all the way.

In his mind, he assumed that this was what she did all the time and that this had been her plan all along. He thought she was so insecure and desperate that she would be willing to do anything to capture and keep the interest of a man. Although he went all the way with her, it left a bad taste in his mouth because he felt it was too easy and that if he could do it, any man could. In actuality, she had been celibate for over a year and was just trying to get back into the swing of dating. She went in not knowing how to position herself and not knowing her true worth. She compromised her deepest beliefs and sent the wrong message to this man. He was somewhat disgusted with the fact that she gave herself to him and also disgusted that he wasn't man enough to stop it before they went all the way. He felt really small because he took advantage of a woman who obviously didn't know her value. If she had let him open the door, he would have. If she had let him pay for the food, he would have. If she had let him drop her off and go on his way, he would have. Instead, because she didn't know her worth, she gave too much and he took what she gave him. Both parties were to blame and both parties carried deep insecurities.

The lesson from that story is that you must know your self-worth prior to entering a relationship. Love yourself so that someone else can love you, too. If you don't know your worth, then you won't get what you're worth. If you lay down, you will get ran over. If you give in, someone may take advantage of you. This woman did not know what she deserved, so she required less and she received less. He wanted to give more but saw that she didn't require more, so he treated her the way he saw her treat herself.

Set the standard for your love and don't compromise. Show others who you are and what you want and stick to it. Never let someone give you less than you deserve or you will always get that. Sometimes you have to be willing to say no so that you can say yes to something far superior. Never let your desperation speak because it is weak and it will produce weak results. Lead by example and others will follow. That is a rule of life, love, and relationships.

~3~
Trust

I f there is no trust, there is no relationship!

Trust is one of the most important parts of a relationship, yet so many people take it for granted. Trust is what strengthens and holds a relationship together. If there is no trust in a relationship, it will slowly begin to corrode. Eventually, the relationship will be stripped bare and there will be nothing left but bitterness, hate, arguments and toxic behavior. Trust is the glue that holds it together. When you trust your partner, it allows you to open yourself up to love and give it all you've got. Trust helps you grow with a person and build on a firm foundation.

It is often said that if a person can't trust you and you've done nothing for them to distrust you, then it is most likely because they can't be trusted. When a person is doing something they know they shouldn't be doing, it always makes them wonder what their partner is doing that they may not know about. That is where the blame game and accusations are birthed. Another thing that prevents trust from being a part of a relationship is insecurity. If a person does not know their worth and they don't love themselves, then they will not understand how anyone else can love them. You'll find that they are overly-sensitive and always needy for words of affirmation that essentially fall on stony ground and don't bear fruit. Insecure people find it very difficult to trust anyone because they expect you to cheat on them or leave them. Therefore, they end up pushing their partners away by constantly questioning their love and loyalty. To a faithful and loyal person, being accused of cheating all the time for no apparent reason will get old really fast. Eventually, the insecure person will drive their faithful partner right out of the relationship. Thus, a lack of trust in a relationship will lead to emotional abuse, which will destroy a relationship for good.

If you don't trust your partner, it's important that you evaluate the reasons why. Be honest with yourself and identify if the problem lies with you or with them. Once trust is lost, it's never fully regained. So if your partner has cheated on you and you can't seem to fully trust them, then it's a sign you should let them go so you both can start over fresh. Not doing so will only lead to more pain and heartache because your accusations will frustrate them and possibly lead them to cheat again in hopes that they will get caught and that you will just leave. If you are going to accuse someone of cheating every day, they would rather you leave them than for you to stay.

It has been said that we should forgive and forget, but we never really forget. Forgiving and forgetting actually means that we should forgive them and then never remind them of the offense. Contrary to that, we often say we've forgiven a person and then remind them of the offense often. That actually means we never really forgave them for hurting us. If you can't forgive and forget, then you need to just forgive and then forget them. It would be easier for you to start over fresh after being deceived than to force it to work knowing that you will be hurting every day for the rest of your life.

So often people hold onto a dying relationship, trying to revive it, only to find out that they almost died with it. Life is too short to live and die for someone who is not willing to do the same for you. When a person loses your trust, they are indirectly telling you that they don't respect you and that they are not ready for a real relationship. When a person tells you that through their actions, believe them! Take heed to the messages they are sending your way or you will pay a great price in the long run.

There was once a guy who cheated on every girlfriend he ever had. He was a smooth talker and a smooth walker. He was a ladies' man and could pretty much get any lady he wanted. He wasn't really ready for real love or a real relationship but he wouldn't tell these women that. He made them believe that he was Mister Perfect and that he wanted each one of them to be his wife. That way, they would open up and give him their all. He would have three to four women open at the same time and he was weighing his options, looking for the one that he might give a chance. Does this guy sound familiar? When he would actually make it official with a woman, it was never long before he would cheat. Each time, his conscience always got the best of him and he would confess his offenses. He always suspected that they were cheating because he was cheating. With every situation in which he cheated, he believed that his women would do the same if they were put in those same scenarios. He could have been right or he could have been wrong, but either way, his insecurities would always speak louder than his mouth.

He would admit his infidelities to them and then tell them to deal with it or leave. He would rather them leave than to stay because he felt that once the trust was lost, it could never be restored. So the purpose of his cheating was essentially to tell them that he didn't want to be with them. His confessing was done to confirm any notion they may have had. His biggest fear was that they would cheat on him and he would be unable to stomach the taste of his own medicine. So rather than waiting on what he felt was inevitable, he would try everything in his power to push them away. What's odd is that he would hurt them but he didn't want to be hurt back. He would ask for their trust but he didn't trust them, nor did he trust himself. Because of this behavior, he practically ruined every relationship he ever entered. Ironically, many of the women who were victims of his cheating wanted to stay with him anyway. If they didn't leave, he would let them stay, but that wouldn't change his behavior. He would continue to cheat because he figured they were only staying out of convenience and the desire for revenge. Whether that was true or not, he was not concerned with finding out. He continued to do what he had always done, which was cheat.

One day he met his match. He began a relationship with a young lady and he began cheating on her. For some reason, this time he thought that he could cheat, admit it to her and still expect her not to even the score. He felt that he was "God's gift" to her and that she needed him and would never retaliate. He dropped his guard on this young lady and took her for granted. After he cheated, she lost all trust in him but she didn't leave. She figured she would be with him and they just wouldn't trust each other. She assumed that both of them would simply continue to live the same lifestyle, like an open relationship. He didn't get the memo. He thought he was allowed to cheat and that her role was to just sit around and wait for him to return to the dorm when he was finished. For some strange reason, he trusted her with all his heart. She had proven herself to be faithful and loyal, and he bought into it. His karma train was on its way though. Since she didn't trust him, she decided that she would sleep around also. She began sleeping with his teammates and friends, but unlike him, she wouldn't confess to it. She held onto the secret for her own satisfaction. Eventually, his team started telling him that they suspected she was cheating and they suggested that he investigate. He doubted it and told them they were crazy, but just to be sure, he checked in with her about it. After hours of questioning, she finally owned up to her wrongdoing. She admitted to a different guy each day until eventually she had confessed to cheating with five different men. To say the least, he was shocked and appalled. He was blown away that what he had always done to women had finally backfired on him. He cried himself to sleep for many nights and he hurt like never before. The karma train had made its stop!

That story paints a picture of what happens when trust is lost in a relationship. It typically heads downhill. There are exceptions to every rule, and right now someone reading this believes they are that exception. That's fine to believe, especially if it turns out to be true! Unfortunately, it simply does not end up that way in most cases. When trust is gone, everything else in the relationship begins to fade also. Each part of a relationship depends on trust to be the glue, and without it there isn't much left. So if you happen to be fortunate enough to be single or in a relationship where the trust is still intact, please remember what you have just read. It will save you a lot of heartache! Trust can go a long way!

❧4❧

Honesty

A lie never solves the problem; it just makes it a bigger problem that you'll have to deal with later.

Honesty goes hand-in-hand with trust. Trust is lost because a person isn't being honest. So to have trust in a relationship, both parties must be honest. Without honesty, there is no trust and without trust, there will be no honesty. One comes with the other and the two make a happy and healthy relationship that is centered and balanced.

Why do people lie?

One of the main reasons people lie is because of fear. They fear the consequences of their actions, and they feel that telling a lie will allow them to escape those consequences. The ability to lie is natural for some and learned for others. It starts in childhood. Kids learn how to lie by watching a parent or sibling do one thing and then tell someone else that they did another thing. Right there a lie has been birthed and passed down all at once. Now this child believes that it is acceptable or normal to lie about something when they do not want to reveal what really happened.

The natural liars are actually taught also, but they learned in a different way. A natural liar is someone who received excessive punishment for transgression early on in life and to avoid that pain, began lying to escape those consequences. That pattern transfers into adulthood and eventually these people find themselves lying about almost everything, even when the consequences aren't extreme.

When we fear the outcome of something, lies provide an escape, a temporary one at least. A lie will always catch up to you! People cheat and then lie because they don't want to lose the person they have. They want to be able to do wrong and not be punished. It's comparable to if a child did something wrong and then took off running when the time came for a spanking or time-out. Why cheat if you don't want to lose your significant other? That's a book in itself!

A lack of honesty in a relationship is like termite infestation in a house; eventually it will be ruined beyond repair. Concerning lies, you should have a 3-strike rule. The reason for this is to give a person a chance to grow and change, because people can change. However, don't ever settle for playing the fool for too long or you will always be taken for granted. What you reinforce is what will repeat itself. Therefore, if a person lies to you and you allow them to continue telling lie after lie, they will never have any motivation to change the behavior. Before you know it, you will fall in too deep and feel that you can never leave them.

Analyze why the person is lying and be sure that you are not forcing them to lie because they don't feel safe in the relationship. There was once a young lady who tried her best to do right by her boyfriend, but as humans occasionally do at times, she would fall short in that area. If a guy from the past who was only a friend called her out the blue, she would tell her boyfriend to save any trouble. She wanted to tell her boyfriend just in case he saw the call log in her phone one day. If that happened, he wouldn't overreact because she would have already given him a heads-up about her friend. However, because she told him about something in the past, he would flip out to the point that she was afraid of him. At this point, she felt she couldn't even tell him about very small things that would occur. The reason is because he didn't make her feel safe. He would react excessively over trivial things such as a guy looking at her or saying hello and her being polite and speaking back. He constantly questioned her whereabouts as if he was her parole officer. He invaded her privacy and disrespected her as a person. This created a hostile environment and she didn't feel that he would understand about the little things. Therefore she chose to lie. The lies didn't help anything because he usually found out and flipped out even more. One issue led to another and the problems just began to pile up one by one. Eventually their relationship evolved into too much for either to handle and they split up. If he had been mature and secure, he would have realized that she is human and could not control the occasional run-ins with the opposite sex. His maturity would have prevented her need to lie in order to cushion his insecurities, and they could have built something special together.

If you are a liar, it is imperative that you confront yourself right now. Evaluate your past and reason with yourself to find out why you lie. Get to the root of the problem and then pluck it of your life. Understand today that lies will not help your relationship or save you any trouble; they will actually cause the opposite. Trust and know that the truth is the best way to go. If a person cannot handle your truth, then that is a clear sign that they are not the person for you. There is no need to lie, and if you feel the need to do so, then that's a red flag which should not be ignored. Have no fear! We only lie when we fear the consequences, so if you fear the consequences of a particular action, then don't act! It's not rocket science when it concerns being honest. You just have to do it and trust that in the long run, it will work out in your favor. Liars don't last, lovers do.

Don't let lies break down what you are trying to build. Lying is a bad habit and really hard to break. Don't allow yourself to get caught up in the vicious cycle of lying; it can ruin your relationship and your life.

≈5≈

Affection

A ffection is a very important part of a relationship. We all need to feel the love that is professed to us. It's not enough for someone to just tell us they love us every day. We need to feel their touch, their hug, their kiss, and their love. The physical touch expresses love in a way that words cannot. There are different types of affection and different ways that affection should be shown to each gender. A man does not want the same type of affection that a woman may desire and vice versa. It is important to understand what affection really is and how to show it.

For the ladies:

Affection is important for guys just as it is for you, but men typically like affection in a different manner than women. You may want to hold hands or cuddle for hours or kiss a lot, whereas a man may want to do those things too, but for a much shorter time. Men love to feel your touch, like a gentle rub of his face, scratching his head and rubbing his back. It almost sounds like you're petting a dog, doesn't it? Hmm interesting! Ironically, many women do refer to men as "dogs."

It is important to let your man feel your touch. It lets him know that you love him and that you care. It makes him feel safe and warm on the inside even though he may never verbalize that. Most men have a certain comfort level where they must remain. They don't like stepping outside of that comfort zone because it makes them feel vulnerable and less than a man. Unless sex is to follow, most men do not like long passionate kissing. Hence the phrase, *a man will be intimate for sex and a woman will have sex for intimacy.* That phrase explains it perfectly. It's not fair, but it's fact. Another thing that makes most men a little uncomfortable is holding hands for long periods of times in public. Unless a man has really matured, holding hands will make him feel a little uneasy or "soft." Any form of public display of affection will make most men feel a little mushy in a way that may make them uncomfortable.

It's important that you remember that different people like to be loved in different ways. You may have a man who loves doing all of those things listed above and you are the opposite. That's possible also, as there is always an exception to the rule. But understand that a man may not like the things you like, so it's important to find out what he does like and then do those things or communicate to him and see if you all can meet in the middle. Example, if you love holding hands while you're walking and he hates it, see if he is comfortable with holding hands for five minutes on and five minutes off. That way, you both are getting what you need and should both be happy. If you love kissing and he doesn't, see if he will be comfortable kissing in private whenever you want and you promise that you won't make him kiss in public. If he wants sex and you want kissing, but neither of you wants what the other wants, you should agree not to do either. It's not fair for you to demand a long passionate kiss and get your fix and then expect him to be happy with it if he doesn't get what he wants from it. If you play with fire you, will get burned! So find out what makes you both happy and then find a happy medium. If you are selfish and determined to love only the way you want to love and refuse to respect how he wants to love, then you will get left behind. If you make a man feel uncomfortable for too long, he would rather leave than bear that feeling forever. Be mindful of that risk.

Please do not mistake sex for love, or sex for affection. Sex can be an expression of love or it can be an expression of lust. It is up to you to discern which one you are expressing in your relationship. If it's within a hundred hours of talk time with a man, then it's most likely lust. It takes a man much longer to fall in love than it does for a woman. Men are less sensitive and don't register feelings and emotions as much as women. Women analyze things much more than men, and therefore, you magnify your love in a very short amount of time, whereas men are the opposite. It can easily take a man twelve months to feel as strongly about a woman as she felt about him in two months. Therefore, a woman should really think carefully before having sex with a man just because he says that it's his way of showing love. Where real love is present, sex is just a plus, not a priority. There have been many women who gave in to a man's plea for sex before he actually was in love, and that man took her most prized possession and left her not long after. Once you give it away, you cannot get it back, so think long and hard before you take that step.

A man who is truly interested in a woman and sees her as someone he can spend his life with is all about real affection. That man will kiss, hold hands, cuddle or whatever it takes to show her that he really cares. He will open up, step out of his comfort zone and be vulnerable to show her that he is truly in it for the long haul. Ladies, if you have that in a man, take special note of it and don't take it for granted because it is rare. However, just because you shouldn't take it for granted does not mean that you should throw all inhibition out the window. Take your time and let the love grow even stronger. The longer, the stronger. Don't rush it or you will ruin it.

To the Men:

Women are emotional creatures! They need love more than we can imagine. To hold a woman's hand means the world to her. It's gentle, subtle, and caring. It shows her that you are not embarrassed by who is watching and that you only want her to know that you really care. Affection is a love language that almost every woman speaks. A wholesome woman would much rather kiss deeply and passionately than have sex. It shows a woman much more when a man would rather kiss her than have sex with her. She understands that you may have sex with a woman who you don't like, but you don't kiss women you don't like. So keep that in mind when you are trying to show a woman you really like her.

Don't put affection into a sexual box. Affection is much more than that. Please understand that affection can also be seen as just looking deep into her eyes and telling her your every feeling without even speaking a word. If you want to show a woman that you really care for her, then leave sex for last. Do the little things that send her a much stronger message. Spend time with her, talk to her for hours, hold her hand in public, kiss her softly, and kiss her passionately and don't ask for sex. Be a real man and only deal with a woman who you can see yourself with for life. It may take many tries before you find that one, but in that process, don't leave a trail of brokenhearted women because you were not man enough to tell them early on that they weren't the ones for you. Save your affection for that special woman so that when you find her and you give it to her, she will feel special to have you. Don't spread yourself too thin, it's a mistake that men often make!

Don't let sex rule your mind. Instead, go in and give her everything except that and let it be her choice of when you all take it to the next level. That is always the best way to let it flow. A woman is very special to have and you want to have all of her, but on her time. Don't force it or you will push her away.

Hold her hand without her having to initiate it. Take the first step and grab her hand. It will blow her mind because women are aware that holding hands in public is not a man's favorite thing to do.

It takes a real man to step outside of himself and his natural desires and to give a woman what she wants and needs. But for the man who does do that for a deserving woman, he will be richly rewarded with a love that he has never imagined. Women are made for love, but oftentimes that love must be shown to them first before they give their all. When they do, you can rest assure that it will be worth it. So, instead of going in to the relationship trying to get what you can out of it, go in looking to give all that you can. Then allow her to reciprocate and you will learn very quickly that she was born to do this thing called love.

So guys please remember to take your time and to show her genuine and true affection. What you call affection may not be what she calls affection. So, if you don't know, ask her and then give her what she asks of you and you will not regret it. Never be in a rush, it won't help. It will hurt!

~6~

Personal space

Personal space is very essential to a healthy relationship. It allows the two individuals to remain who they are and only come together to complement one another. Both parties should promote personal space in a relationship in order to keep a healthy balance. Trust and honesty will definitely have to be in the relationship for personal space to be allowed. No one wants to give personal space to someone they don't trust because they fear that this person may cheat. That is a problem, but we see it all the time. Personal space for a man and a woman are two different things and they fulfill different things in each person. Then there are also unhealthy individuals who do not want to give any personal space for reasons of their own.

Personal space can be very effective and helpful in a relationship because it allows a person to breathe. It's like stepping away from your job for a moment for a breath of fresh air. Even if your job is enjoyable, it's always good to step away for a moment and then return rejuvenated. When you step away, you are able to clear your head, take some deep breaths and then come back ready and focused. Imagine a painter or sound engineer. They both have fun jobs, but if they work for hours and hours, they can become fatigued, which then affects the quality of their work. The same goes for a relationship; it's work even if it's fun. If you are always in close proximity to your significant other, you are not allowing yourself any room to grow. Personal space is that small break that allows you to regroup, get a breath of fresh air and then return ready.

Personal space for women may be for different purposes than for men. Since most women are made for love, they are able to dwell in the trenches of a relationship longer than a men can; loving is in the nature of a woman. When a woman wants to go out, it's with the girls. She is doing it for girl talk. A happy woman may also want to go out with her girls, just to brag about how good her man is to her. Of course, she won't admit that she's really bragging, but its true most of the time. It's always great for a woman to be able to go out with the girls, especially if she is happy in her relationship because she only returns happier. It adds a level of intensity to the love that already exists.

For a faithful man, personal space is a lot like it is for a faithful woman. A man needs that free time to laugh, jock and hang with the guys. He needs to be able to talk about football teams and games, using all the sports jargon and terminology that his friends comprehend. Truthfully, there are some women who can comprehend and contribute to that sort of talk, but it's still not the same as a conversation with the guys. A man needs that space also because men get bored really easily and that could lead to him cheating. So giving a man that personal space is good because he gets a chance to miss his woman and will come back rejuvenated and wanting more of her. Men also like personal space to just be alone. A lot of men are introverts and may just want some time to themselves. Ever heard of a "man cave?" You may never hear of a "woman cave" because they don't really exist, but a "man cave" does show you that it is necessary. Some men may just want to watch the game in private or sit alone and laugh out loud at a favorite comedian. He just needs some time to get in touch with himself and not feel like he needs a woman present all of the time. This may be hard for a lot of women to understand, but for the women who do, your relationships will operate much more smoothly if you recognize this concept. A man really loves a woman who doesn't try to smother him and is able to find a healthy balance with her affection and her space. This is very important to master because it can make or break a relationship.

Before you can know if personal space will be effective, you first need to know if you have trust and honesty in your relationship. That is very important because if you can't trust your partner, then giving them personal space is a recipe for trouble. It's in that time when cheating really happens in the name of personal space. It is important to know that your partner is honest and trustworthy; otherwise, you are in for a world of problems. It has been common knowledge for quite some time that a cheating partner frequently uses the excuse that they need some personal space to breathe, when in reality they aim to go breathe on someone else! It will take a gut feeling to really know who and what you're working with. Trust your instincts, they are usually right! If you notice the signs of a cheater in your partner, then pay close attention. Don't become paranoid, but do pay attention.

If you feel that your partner may be a cheating or untrustworthy, then you really need to evaluate some things. The personal space you may need to give them is to break up. If you can't trust a person, then you shouldn't be with them. It's that simple. To be with someone who you can't trust with personal space...well, that sounds more like prison doesn't it? That is not a healthy relationship at all. Yet it is somewhat common these days. Make sure that that's not the condition of your relationship. If you have someone who cannot be trusted yet you refrain from discussing it and give him or her personal space, then you are playing yourself. Sometimes it is best to let a person go so that they can grow. Personal space in a relationship is very necessary, but it will only benefit a mature and faithful couple!

There are some individuals who do not like giving their partners any personal space and would rather spend every waking moment with them. That is a clear indication of insecurity and low self-esteem. That is also a red flag for a very toxic relationship. It starts out cute and cuddly, but it soon turns very dangerous. If a person does not trust you and you have given them no reason not to, then you should be worried. It usually means that they can't be trusted themselves.

If you have someone who never wants you to hang out with your friends and always wants to be around you, then it's time to wake up! It is very dangerous because they are telling you that they don't know how to love. When a person doesn't really know who they are or what they are worth or if they've been through a lot of pain in their life, they usually turn out like this. It is dangerous because that person will become very controlling and when they feel that they can no longer control you, they may grow irate or violent, which could lead to dire consequences for both individuals.

If you are in a situation like that, be strong enough to identify that behavior and let it go. It will save your partner and yourself. People who are insecure rarely recognize that it's insecurities which cause them to act that way. They call it love or affection. They try to make you think that they want all of your time because they care so much for you and that everyone else in the world does not have your best interest at heart they way they do. You cannot accept that and you have to be strong enough to walk away if they are unwilling to change and grow. Demand your personal space if you need it and if that person can't handle it, then that's a sign that you should not be with them. If you can trust yourself and you know that you will not cheat on your partner, they you should be able to go out with friends or family whenever you choose to do so. If they have a problem with it, then that is their problem and not yours. Don't let someone come in your life and attempt to change you from who you are unless they are changing you for the better.

It is important that when you go into a relationship, you don't lose your independence. The two of you should become one after marriage, but while dating, you still need to be able to identify with yourself and who you are! If you lose yourself in every relationship you enter, soon there won't be much of you left!

A relationship isn't meant to feel like captivity. Instead, it should feel like true freedom and bliss!

7

Communication 101

Communication to a relationship is like oxygen to life!
You cannot have a healthy relationship without great
communication skills. Communication is what keeps things
afloat. Communication bridges the gap between men and women.
Although communication sometimes fails to be a strong suit for men,
it is necessary that a woman leads her man to that point through some
strategic communication patterns of her own. The more a man expresses himself to a woman, the more he will fall in love. Getting a
man to communicate can be like pulling teeth from a pit bull, but it
can be done!

Women have to understand that men communicate on their own
time and under their own circumstances. The environment has to be
set in the right mood and the conversation must occur at the right
time. If the atmosphere is tense, then a man will be tense. If a man
knows his woman is angry, he will clam up. If this happens, then the
communication that he does present may not be what the woman
wants to hear. Women must be smart about how they communicate
with men.

- Always wait at least an hour to discuss the issue after it's happened. That way, you are cool and can express yourself effectively.

- Use "I feel" statements! Don't point the blame. Just explain how it makes you feel.
- Seek to understand rather than to be understood.
- Take turns talking and listen twice as much as you talk.
- Beware of coercion by fear and manipulation by guilt.
- Don't argue!!
- Don't get caught up in power struggles; side step them, even if it means abandoning the conversation and returning to it later.
- Don't expect a man to be as expressive and articulate as you are. Scientifically, men lack the cognitive skills that women possess.
- Don't curse! It's the precursor to violence and it intensifies the conversation. Be calm enough to express yourself without cursing or insults. If you can't, it's a clear indication that you need more time to cool off.
- Don't allow a man to curse, scream, yell or call you out of your name! Neither should you do any of these things towards him. Be strong enough to walk away from it and come back when you can talk like adults.
- The communication that you reinforce will repeat itself. Don't create bad patterns or habits in your communication because it will ruin your relationship.
- In a time of peace, prepare for war. Talk about things before they arise instead of after the fact. As you've heard, an ounce of prevention is better than a pound of cure.
- Let him communicate at his own pace, but never sweep a serious matter under the rug and expect it to simply disappear.

These issues will only build and eventually you will trip over them.

- The difference between a good and bad relationship is leaving a few things unsaid.

Those are some powerful tips on communication that can make or break your relationship. Men are not built like women and it's important to remember that when communicating. A man has to feel that he has some sense of control over the situation or else he will shut down or lose his cool. By nature, men are "fight or flight" creatures. If backed into a corner, they will either start a fight or take flight. That is not the reaction you want in a relationship. What you want is to be able to get that man to sit down and talk with you, and it will take you using the tips above to your advantage.

We all remember in grade school when females would argue forever and never throw a blow. On the other hand, we would see two guys get into an argument, exchange a few words and then promptly start throwing blows. That's a very vivid example of how men and women communicate differently. Knowing that, we must approach our communication carefully.

The more men and women communicate and open up to one another, the better our relationships will become.

For the men reading this, it's important that you comprehend the creature with which you are dealing. Understand that the average woman speaks 25,000 words a day to your 10,000 words a day. She wants to express herself and be heard, and she wants to hear you. She needs you to open up and tell her what's on your mind and what she can do better. Not only what she can do better, but also what you are going to improve. If you can't find the words, then take some time to put it on paper. Ask her to give you an hour or however long you need to assemble your thoughts together and then return to her with it. She needs to know that you care! When she is speaking, look her in the eyes and watch her like you are watching ESPN. Listen to respond. Ask questions that make her explain more. Give her your undivided attention as often as possible. This is what shows her that you hear her and that you really care!

When it all boils down to it, we must have great communication if we want to have great relationships. Both sexes must learn how to effectively communicate with the opposite sex. Both sides must be willing to grow and go to the next level. If you are unwilling to expand, then you will lose out on the love of your life.

Communicating the right way is never easy initially, but the more you practice, the easier it will become. Love is real and there are very happy relationships all over the world. It's not just a fairytale, but even those happy, successful couples will tell you that they learned how to communicate with one another.

Communication to a relationship is like oxygen to life!

∾8∾

Privacy of your relationship

T reat your relationship like your house, doors locked!

So many relationships have been ruined because one or both partners disclosed just too much personal information about the relationship to others. What you have to realize is that not everyone else will be happy for you. Therefore, they may not give you the best advice. When you are in a relationship, there will be arguments and disagreements. Unless these minor issues are harming you, then they are not anyone else's business. Each time you run and reveal your disagreements to others, they add a strike to your partner's record. Before long, your partner will strike out in the minds of your family and friends, and they will advise you accordingly. Your partner may have made up for those minor transgressions with good behavior, but all your friend knows about are the wrongdoings, not the improvements, so it doesn't count. Now you have a friend who hates your partner and a partner who loves you sincerely. You are torn on whom to give your loyalty because you don't want to lose either. At this point, you probably don't even realize that you are the cause for this rift in the first place. Now that you have created this tension that neither party may be able to get over, something will have to give. One of them will give you an ultimatum and you will have to choose. Perhaps you could try to bring them together and resolve the issue…but that very rarely works. In order to solve the issue, you would have to bring the two of them together and admit fault. You would have to admit that your disagreements were not detrimental and that you were wrong to discuss them outside of the relationship. You would have to admit that you were seeking attention or sympathy from both sides to compensate for your lack of self-esteem. You will have to mature in the very moment and accept the blame for driving this wedge between your loved ones. If you are going to report the bad, then you need to report the good too, but the good is typically left unsaid.

There was once a young lady who was in a relationship with a guy while they were both trying to figure love out. They had a ton of fun together, laughing, joking and just having a blast. Occasionally, a disagreement would arise, and they would find themselves in a heated argument. There was never violence, just words being exchanged that could sting a little. The young man chose to keep it in house and deal with it between them. The young lady, however, exposed the information to her friend and painted a very ugly picture of her guy. Then she would return to her guy and make up. The cycle repeated itself over and over again just like any typical relationship between two young lovers. Each time, the young lady would go tell her friend and in turn, her friend would build a little more resentment for her friend's boyfriend.

One day, things came to a head. The young lady and her boyfriend got into a small disagreement and the young lady repeated her habit of disclosing it to her friend. This time, the young man went to confront his girlfriend with the intention of sorting things out. His girlfriend coincidentally happened to be with the same friend to whom she disclosed all the negative details of their relationship. Things got out of hand and the friend made it known to the boyfriend that his girlfriend supposedly hated him and was unhappy in her relationship with him. This was news to the boyfriend because his girlfriend had never expressed these sentiments to him. They laughed and joked everyday as if all was well, but obviously something was off. So, the boyfriend confronted the girlfriend about this in front of her friend. At this moment, the girlfriend had to make a choice. She sided with her friend and told her boyfriend to his face that she was unhappy. In truth, what she said was not actually true. She simply said this to save face because she didn't want her friend to discover that she had been blowing things out of proportion for sympathy and sometimes just to have something to talk about. The girlfriend was playing the middle and both ends, and eventually, it blew up in her face.

After the girlfriend left and reflected on what happened, she realized that what she'd been doing all along was wrong and she had to make it right. She had to choose what was more important to her, a friend or the love of her life. She chose the love of her life. She went to him and apologized for divulging every little detail of their relationship to her friend. She also apologized for failing to be open and honest with him. She expressed regret for the confusion and the chaos. This was not good enough for the boyfriend. He felt as if her friend had been playing devil's advocate and was a hindrance to their relationship. As a result, he produced an ultimatum; he demanded that his girlfriend cut her friend off if she wanted to be with him. Although she knew it would be difficult, the girlfriend agreed to do it. She could never really admit to her friend why she had to go her separate way because it would be both hurtful and embarrassing. Instead, she began ignoring her friend and cut her off cold turkey.

She had to face the consequence of losing her best friend, all because she didn't protect her relationship. She tried to play the middle and both ends and got played. Her friend was only intending to be a good friend. The girlfriend was taking all of her problems to her friend, and her friend was merely responding to them. Then when it came down to it, she was forced to choose her man over her friend. Unfortunately, her friend had to lose a friend just for being a good friend.

Remember that story when you feel like discussing everything that happens in your relationship. If it's not worth breaking up over, then it's not worth talking about with others. Unless you are seeking help from people, don't go to them just for the sake of complaining. You will only blow things out of proportion, and in turn, make it worse for yourself. Things will hit the fan at some point and you will be the one who has to bear it. You may fall in and out of love with your partner as the two of you are growing and maturing, but others may never fall in love with your partner at all. Therefore, if you run and tell them all the negativity that is going on, then they have only negative information to use when forming an opinion about your partner.

Treat your relationship like a home, doors locked, unless it starts to burn down!

≈9≈

Importance of religion and faith in successful relationships

T here are all kinds of religions, and for most people, religion is very important in a successful relationship. There are a lot of relationships, but not many are successful. Typically, the successful ones include an element bigger than both individuals, and that is usually religion or faith. Faith comes in the individuals need guidance or strength beyond themselves. Most religions have instructions on relationships and/or marriage that a couple can turn to when needed. Relationships are built on a certain foundation that allows the couple to develop and have guidelines by which to live.

Most of the time, our lives are governed by our morals and values. Naturally, those are found in our religion or faith. If a person does not have anything that they believe in, then what will govern their life? There are atheists, but even atheists have beliefs and faith that govern their lives. If they didn't, then our prison system would be overflowing with atheists, but it's not! There are many men who are Christian who proclaim faithfulness not just to their wives, but to their God. That provides an extra sense of security for a woman; she knows that even though she isn't perfect, she has some assurance based on her man's belief in something greater than himself. On the other hand, if that man fears nothing or answers to nothing, then what will govern his actions? If he does not fear consequences, then what will prevent him from doing the unforgivable to his woman? The same goes for women. That is why faith is a key factor to many relationships.

Everything we know about this life is governed by rules and regulations. In school, on the job, and in society, there are endless rules. Those rules are what keep us in line and ensure that we have a sense of morals. Where there are no rules, there will be chaos. Religion and faith provide the rules that impede relationship chaos. Most religions tell us that we cannot mistreat others, so we treat them how we want to be treated.

We all should answer to something greater than ourselves because when we feel like we are invincible, life shows us that we aren't. When we have something to believe in, it makes life worth living.

Religion can present problems in a relationship when the two individuals practice two different religions. Our religion becomes the core of who we really are. We identify with it, appreciate it and live by it. Some are even willing to die for these beliefs. A person who feels that strongly about something won't compromise it for anyone, but many times people rush into relationships and don't weigh the consequences of standing on different foundations.

There once was a couple who met in college. In truth, the guy just wanted to have a girlfriend, but he was apprehensive about approaching her with that upfront, so he played the friend role. He knew that she was a Christian and he was a Muslim, but he dealt with it because he just wanted a girlfriend. After a few months, they decided to be more than friends and become a couple. The female was not a devout Christian; she had simply been born into the religion.

Although the guy was born into his religion also, he took it seriously. Eventually, they began to grow closer and the guy started putting his foot down and trying to pull rank in her life. They were gaining serious feelings for one another, but at the core, they had different belief systems. He did not believe that Jesus was the son of God, but she did. He wanted to go to the mosque for service, but she wanted to go to the church. She believed that the only way to get into heaven is to accept Jesus Christ as your savior but he didn't believe that. As you can see, they were separated at the core but had never taken the issue into consideration. His will was stronger than hers and he was much more serious about his religious conviction that she was about hers.

He gave her an ultimatum. He preached to her everyday and coerced her into converting. When he went to meet her parents, he criticized the beliefs that they had passed down to her and he stood on his faith without wavering. Her parents were not fond of him or his opinions. They perceived his way of professing his faith as overbearing and rude. Her parents desired for her to remain Christian and to live the way she was taught to live. He wanted her to convert, and he threatened to leave her. Initially, she believed they could maintain their separate religions and make the relationship work. She imagined having a mixed wedding fused with traditions from both sides and raise their kids in a way that they would choose from themselves. He felt that it wasn't logical to allow children who know nothing about life or the world to choose which religion they wanted to follow. Undoubtedly, the children would aim to please both of their parents and would find themselves torn on which religion they should choose. He did not want his kids to grow up confused and torn. He didn't want to have to split up on Sundays with half the family going one place to worship and the other half going somewhere else. He wanted one foundation on which they could build and rely. She wanted the opposite.

Naturally, this caused problems. In order for this to work, someone would have to compromise their convictions. The two belief systems were simply too conflicting at the core; one believed that Jesus was the way and the other believed that Jesus was merely just a prophetic man. How could they possibly serve the same God? Eventually, she very reluctantly converted to Islam. She was not passionate about the teachings or the Quran, nor did she want to be a part of the practices, but she compromised in the name of love. Although she changed, it didn't improve things because she still made mistakes and he wanted her to be perfect. The relationship teachings in his religion were unlike what she was accustomed to and she found herself growing more and more discontented. They constantly fought and argued about which religion was the "real" religion. They would argue about which religion was founded first and which religion has the most credibility. This drove a wedge in between them, and the relationship was no longer about love. They magnified their differences and that became everything to them.

After a couple years of trying to make something out of nothing, this couple began to grow apart. The guy began to realize that he forced her to change by threatening to leave her. His conscience began to get the best of him and he realized that their relationship was not based on real love. By this time, he had pushed her away because of his selfish ways, and they separated. In the end, it was their religious differences that divided them and drove them apart. It's ironic how something that is supposed to bring us together can also separate us.

It's up to the individuals to decide if they are willing to compromise their beliefs, but that does not ensure happiness.

When a couple shares the same religion, they can pray together, go to church together, raise their children with the same philosophy and hold one another accountable. They have the same foundation and they can build something that can stand strong and not give way to the trials and tribulations of life. This may not be vital to everyone, but studies show that couples that pray together, stay together.

⇜10⇝
Making the Most of Single Life

S ingle doesn't always mean lonely and relationship doesn't always mean happy! ~Tony Gaskins Jr.

The single life is supposed to be a beautiful time. Single life is to serve a very specific purpose and that is to get you ready for real love! Being single isn't a curse; it's a blessing in disguise. Life happens in seasons. You have to appreciate the current season and make the best of it. Don't waste the time you have by longing for something that you don't have. Instead, focus on yourself and get your life in line so that you can attract the love of your life.

The blessing of single life is that you can focus all of your energy on yourself. There are no concerns about arguing, getting to know someone else, the ups and downs of relationships, and the extra drama. If you take advantage of this time, you will personally improve yourself in ways that will attract some one on the same level.

Things you should accomplish while single:

1. Work on you: Get in shape! Work on your body and your health. Get a diet plan and a workout plan. Get in the best shape of your life! If you want to attract the opposite sex, then you have to look attractable. If you have to hire a trainer and a stylist, do so. Make sure that you are at your best! Once you are at your best, the rest will come to you.

2. Identify your gifts and passions: Find out what makes you come alive. Pay attention to things you love to do and things that others cannot do as easy as you. Your gifts and passions serve a purpose and were given to you for a reason. Write them down and then began pursuing perfection in those areas.

3. Set Goals: Set personal goals for yourself. You should always be moving onward and upward with goals. Keep your goals in front of you and when it seems like you are getting close to one, set another.

4. Make a plan: After you have identified where you want to go, map out how you are going to get there. There should always be a road map for the road to destiny. It may not be exact, but it will at least keep you on track!

5. Heal before you deal: Take the time to meet with a relationship coach and analyze your past relationship(s.) Learn what you did wrong and what you plan to do differently. Forgive your ex as well as yourself and then take time until the pain goes away. Time heals all things!

Those are 5 easy tasks to complete while you are single! It's very important that you work on yourself before you enter another relationship. So often people look for others to complete them when in all actuality, another person should only be able to complement you. Your goal is to become as complete as you can be so that you do not become dependent on your partner. There are many people who jump from relationship to relationship and never take any time to heal. They keep opening and infecting the same wounds over and over again. Not only do they get hurt, but they hurt others because they are hurting. As we hear all the time, hurt people hurt people! So it is a key step to get healthy before you enter into a relationship. If you are healthy, then it's easier to recognize someone else who is sick, but if you are not healthy, then you won't be able to tell if they are either. Two broken and empty people in a relationship can be a nightmare and you don't want that to be you.

It's important that while you are single you don't become desperate. Desperation is a weak emotion and it produces weak results! Being desperate influences a woman to wear revealing clothing and give in too easily. Desperation is a woman's enemy. A man can always tell when a single woman is desperate for love. He is not attracted nor does he have any sympathy for a desperate woman. Instead, most men will take advantage of such situations just because they can. That does not justify or make it right, but you cannot expect anyone to be responsible for you if you fail to be responsible for yourself. A man can smell desperation a mile away. He will sell you a dream and make you think that a special connection exists between the two of you, and then he will sleep with you until he's tired of you. Then he will leave you high and dry. So many single, desperate women wander from man to man, having sexual relations with each of them because they believe that each of them is "the one," completely unaware that he never intended to stay. Be patient! Be firm! Take your time! Know that if a man is for you, then he is for you and nothing will push him away. A man who is really into you will not leave you just because you won't have sex with him. Instead, he will wait to marry you so that he can have all of you. A real man wants a single woman who knows who she is, what she wants, and where she is going! He wants a woman who is confident but not conceited. He wants a woman who is friendly, but not flirtatious. He wants a woman who is easy-going, but not "easy." Being single is not a curse; it's a blessing. It's the greatest me-time you can have. A relationship is like a job from which you cannot retire. This doesn't mean that it's a bad job, but it does require you to put in work every day. So, appreciate the life you have now and know that one day, you will be able to experience a relationship that is fulfilling and plentiful!

Note from the Author

Thank you for reading this book. The subject of love is so complex, but the aim was to simply touch on the basics of key relationship topics. We hope that you were able to receive something useful from this book, even if it was just one section. When it comes to love and relationships, one lesson could be the difference between life and death. Relationships are very serious and have to be treated as such!

Keep this book with you as a hand guide and read it over and over again. What you read was not just mere opinion; it is insight from years of relationship coaching. It is sound and healthy advice based on real life stories. Each story you read was a real story and teaches real lessons.

For any additional questions or one-on-one relationship coaching, please contact Celebrity Relationship Coach at **advice@TonyGaskins. com** and put this book title in the subject line to receive discounted coaching sessions!

Thanks again for reading!!

Made in the USA
Lexington, KY
21 November 2011